MW00958498

Teacher Guide and Lesson Plans for

The One and Only Ivan

By:

John Pennington

Cover Image by Pixabay.com

The lessons on demand series is designed to provide ready to use resources for novel study. In this book you will find key vocabulary, student organizer pages, and assessments. This guide is divided into two sections. Section one is the teacher section which consists of vocabulary and activities. Section two holds all of the student pages, including assessments and graphic organizers.

Now available! Student Workbooks!

Find them on Amazon.com

Look for bound print editions on Amazon.com

PDF versions can be found on Teacherspayteachers.com

Have a question? Contact me @ Johndavidpennington@yahoo.com

Section One

Teacher Pages

Vocabulary

Suggested Activities

Glossary—Bob and Julia Vocabulary

Patient

Imagination

Ponder

Canopy

Precision

Crevices

Unadorned

Undaunted

Parasites

Digestion

Migrate

Forage

Glossary—Bob and Julia Activities

Reading Check Question / Quiz:

Who owns the animals? Mack

What is the name of their home? The Big Top Mall and Video Arcade

What is wrong with Stella? She is suffering from a wound in her leg

What does Ivan and Julia have in common? They are artists

Blooms Higher Order Question:

Interpret the meaning of "It is never to late to be what you might have been." - George Eliot. How do you think it will show up in the story?

Suggested Activity Sheets (see Section Two):

Character Sketch—Ivan

Character Sketch—Stella

Research Connection—Picasso

Compare and Contrast—Three Visitors and My Visitors Return

Draw the Scene

Mack—Crying Vocabulary

Domain

Harmonica

Amends

Dignified

Heritage

Opportunity

Responsibility

Emphasize

Contemplating

Mesmerized

Unpredictable

Addled

Mack—Crying Activities

Reading Check Question / Quiz:

What does Ivan find to draw with his black crayon? A beetle

Who is the new arrival to the Big Top Mall? Ruby

What does Ivan promise Stella? That he will get Ruby to a safe place

What happens to Stella? She dies from the wound in her leg

Blooms Higher Order Question:

Design the perfect habitat for an animal (your choice of animal). It must include a minimum of five features designed specifically for the animals benefit.

Suggested Activity Sheets (see Section Two):

Character Sketch—Mack

Character Sketch—Ruby

Research Connection—Circus

Lost Scene—Write a scene that could have taken place in the story

Advertisement—The Big Top Mall and Video Arcade

The One and Only Ivan—Finally Vocabulary

Nimble

Tolerant

Venture

Revenge

Temperamental

Trudge

The One and Only Ivan—Finally Activities

Reading Check Question / Quiz:

What is the name of Ivan's sister? Tag (Not-Tag stuffed animal)

Ivan stops using the word domain and begins using _____? Cage

Where does Ivan decide Ruby needs to go for her safety? Zoo

Why is it difficult to read Ivan's painting? Made of several small sheets to make a bulletin board size painting.

Blooms Higher Order Question:

Drawn an picture on 16 sheets of paper like Ivan. Shuffle the stack and give to another person. How much time does it take for them to understand the picture? Record how long it takes for several people if you have time.

Suggested Activity Sheets (see Section Two):

Character Sketch— Bob

Character Sketch—George

Research Connection—Africa

Precognition Sheet—What will happen next?

What Would You Do?

The Next Morning—Silverback Vocabulary

Suspiciously

Impossible

Curious

Distinguished

Patient

Protest

Inspect

Property

Associate

Lumber

Loam

Juvenile

The Next Morning—Silverback Activities

Reading Check Question:

Who pushed for a change of habitat for all the animals at the Mall? The protesters, Inspectors

How did they try and get the animals into cages? Lure them with food

What happened to Ivan and Ruby? They ended up in a zoo

What happened to Bob? Living with George and Julia

Blooms Higher Order Question:

Research and defend the value of a Zoo. Are they good places for animals? Why should we have or not have them.

Suggested Activity Sheets (see Section Two):

Character Sketch—Maya

Character Sketch—Kinyani

Create the Test

Top Ten List—Animals that you would save that are endangered

Sequencing—Major events in the story

Chapter Vocabulary

Chapter Activities

Reading Check Question:

Blooms Higher Order Question:

Suggested Activity Sheets (see Section Two):

Important Characters/Places/Things:

Section Two

Student Work Pages

Work Pages

Graphic Organizers

Assessments

Activity Descriptions

Advertisement—Select an item from the text and have the students use text clues to draw an advertisement about that item.

Chapter to Poem—Students select 20 words from the text to write a five line poem with 3 words on each line.

Character Sketch—Students complete the information about a character using text clues.

Comic Strip— Students will create a visual representation of the chapter in a series of drawings.

Compare and Contrast—Select two items to make relationship connections with text support.

Create the Test—have the students use the text to create appropriate test questions.

Draw the Scene—students use text clues to draw a visual representation of the chapter.

Interview— Students design questions you would ask a character in the book and then write that characters response.

Lost Scene—Students use text clues to decide what would happen after a certain place in the story.

Making Connections—students use the text to find two items that are connected and label what kind of relationship connects them.

Precognition Sheet—students envision a character, think about what will happen next, and then determine what the result of that would be.

Activity Descriptions

Pyramid—Students use the text to arrange a series of items in an hierarchy format.

Research Connection—Students use an outside source to learn more about a topic in the text.

Sequencing—students will arrange events in the text in order given a specific context.

Support This! - Students use text to support a specific idea or concept.

Travel Brochure—Students use information in the text to create an informational text about the location

Top Ten List—Students create a list of items ranked from 1 to 10 with a specific theme.

Vocabulary Box—Students explore certain vocabulary words used in the text.

What Would You Do? - Students compare how characters in the text would react and compare that with how they personally would react.

Who, What, When, Where, and How—Students create a series of questions that begin with the following words that are connected to the text.

Write a Letter—Students write a letter to a character in the text.

Activity Descriptions (for scripts and poems)

Add a Character—Students will add a character that does not appear in the scene and create dialog and responses from other characters.

Costume Design—Students will design costumes that are appropriate to the characters in the scene and explain why they chose the design.

Props Needed— Students will make a list of props they believe are needed and justify their choices with text.

Soundtrack! - Students will create a sound track they believe fits the play and justify each song choice.

Stage Directions— Students will decide how the characters should move on, around, or off stage.

Poetry Analysis—Students will determine the plot, theme, setting, subject, tone and important words and phrases.

NAME:

TEACHER:

Date:

Advertisement: Draw an advertisement for _____

Chapter to Poem

Assignment: Select 20 words found in the chapter to create a poem where each line is 3 words long.

Title:

_____   _____   _____

_____   _____   _____

_____   _____   _____

_____   _____   _____

_____   _____   _____

NAME:

TEACHER:

Date:

Character Sketch

Name

Personality/ Distinguishing marks

Draw a picture

Connections to other characters

Important Actions

NAME:

TEACHER:

Date:

Comic Strip

Compare and Contrast

Venn Diagram

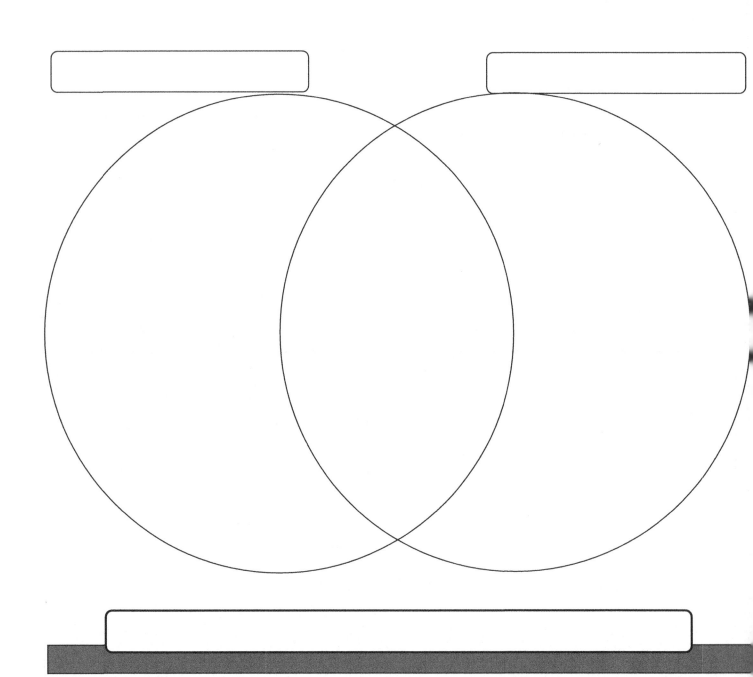

Create the Test

Question:

Answer:

Question:

Answer:

Question:

Answer:

Question:

Answer:

Draw the Scene: What five things have you included in the scene?

1

2

3

4

5

NAME:

TEACHER:

Date:

Interview: Who _____

Question:

Answer:

Question:

Answer:

Question:

Answer:

Question:

Answer:

Lost Scene: Write a scene that takes place between _____ and _____

NAME:

TEACHER:

Date:

Making Connections

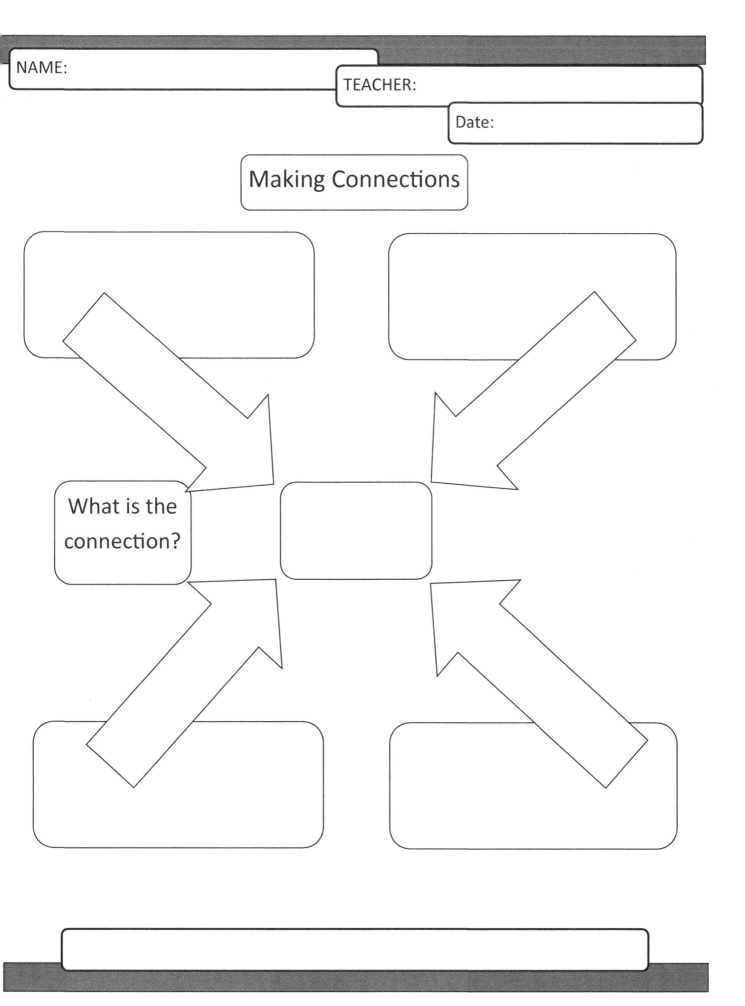

What is the connection?

NAME:

TEACHER:

Date:

Precognition Sheet

Who ?

What's going to happen?

What will be the result?

Who ?

What's going to happen?

What will be the result?

Who ?

What's going to happen?

What will be the result?

Who ?

What's going to happen?

What will be the result?

How many did you get correct?

Assignment: Pyramid

NAME:

TEACHER:

Date:

Research connections

Source (URL, Book, Magazine, Interview)

What am I researching?

Facts I found that could be useful or notes

1.

2.

3.

4.

5.

6.

1.

2.

3.

4.

5.

Sequencing
or timeline

Support This!

Supporting text

What page?

Supporting text

What page?

Central idea or statement

_____

Supporting text

What page?

Supporting text

What page?

NAME:

TEACHER:

Date:

Travel Brochure

Why should you visit?

What are you going to see?

Map

Special Events

NAME:

TEACHER:

Date:

Top Ten List

1.

2.

3.

4.

5.

6.

7.

8.

9.

10.

NAME:

TEACHER:

Date:

Vocabulary Box

Definition:

Draw:

Word:

Related words:

Use in a sentence:

Definition:

Draw:

Word:

Related words:

Use in a sentence:

NAME:

TEACHER:

Date:

What would you do?

Character: _____

What did they do?

Example from text:

What would you do?

Why would that be better?

Character: _____

What did they do?

Example from text:

What would you do?

Why would that be better?

Character: _____

What did they do?

Example from text:

What would you do?

Why would that be better?

NAME:

TEACHER:

Date:

Who, What, When, Where, and How

Who

What

Where

When

How

NAME:

TEACHER:

Date:

Write a letter

To:

From:

NAME:

TEACHER:

Date:

Assignment:

Add a Character

Who is the new character?

What reason does the new character have for being there?

Write a dialog between the new character and characters currently in the scene.

You dialog must be 6 lines or more, and can occur in the beginning, middle or end of the scene.

Costume Design

Draw a costume for one the characters in the scene.

Why do you believe this character should have a costume like this?

NAME:

TEACHER:

Date:

Props Needed

Prop:

What text from the scene supports this?

Prop:

What text from the scene supports this?

Prop:

What text from the scene supports this?

NAME:

TEACHER:

Date:

Soundtrack!

Song:

Why should this song be used?

Song:

Why should this song be used?

Song:

Why should this song be used?

NAME:

TEACHER:

Date:

Stage Directions

List who is moving, how they are moving and use text from the dialog to determine when they move.

Who:

How:

When:

Who:

How:

When:

Who:

How:

When:

NAME:

TEACHER:

Poetry Analysis

Date:

Name of Poem:

Subject:

Text Support:

Plot:

Text Support:

Theme:

Text Support:

Setting:

Text Support:

Tone:

Text Support:

Important Words and Phrases:

Why are these words and phrases important:

Made in United States
North Haven, CT
04 October 2024